Pause Point

How to Reclaim Your Time and Live a More Fulfilling Life

By

Wynne Stephenson

Disclaimer

Copyright © by Wynne Stephenson 2023. All rights reserved. Before this document is duplicated or reproduced in any manner, the publisher's consent must be gained. Therefore, the contents within can neither be stored electronically, transferred, nor kept in a database. Neither part nor full can the document be copied, scanned, faxed, or retained without approval from the publisher or creator.

Table of contents

Introduction

Do you ever feel as if you're never quite enough?

As if there's never enough time in a day to accomplish everything? And do you remain unhappy even after you've finished your to-do list?

Then you are not alone yourself. It's easy to get caught up in the everyday hubbub in today's fast-paced world. Messages suggesting us we should be doing more, accomplishing more, and having it all are incessantly hurled at us. In truth, however, we don't need everything to have happy and satisfied lives. In fact, learning to pause could contain the answer to live a more satisfying life.

I'll show you how to take tiny pauses throughout the day to recover your time and lead a more meaningful life in this book. A pause point is basically a planned time when you take a break from your present work to think about your priorities and take stock of your well-being.

Taking a minute to pause and think about what's important to you enables you to better understand your wants and desires and guarantees that your time and energy are being focused on the things that truly matter. Pauses may be extensive or short, professional or informal. They may be eaten by themselves or in groups. Finding what works for you is vital, as is keeping consistency in your practice.

We'll explore a number of methods and ideas for stopping throughout the day in the upcoming chapters. I'll also speak about the benefits of taking pauses and how they may make your life more fulfilling. Hitting pauses may help you reconnect with yourself and live a life that is more in keeping with your values and aims, whether you're feeling anxious, stressed, or simply lost. Take a minute to pause now as a beginning point.

How do you feel right now?

What wants and needs do you have?

What is one action you can perform right now to come closer to your objectives?

You may begin to design a pause point routine that works for you when you have a greater idea of who you are and what you seek. Increase the amount of time you spend taking stops each day by beginning small and working your way up. As you grow more acclimated to taking pauses, you'll realize benefits throughout your entire life. You'll have greater satisfaction, productivity, and less stress.

Thus, why do you delay?

Let's down to it

Chapter 1

What's the Point of Pause?

Our workplace is fast-paced and packed with stimuli all the time. Since we are constantly expected to be working, it could be tough to find time for rest and relaxation. A plethora of concerns, such as stress, anxiety, and burnout, may emerge from this.

A "Pause Point" is a term used to describe a period or position in life when individuals actively stop, step back, and contemplate. It's a purposeful decision to take a break from the frantic routine of daily activities in order to have some time for meditation and idleness. A Pause Point is a planned respite in the busy pace of life that allows an opportunity to review what essential, practice mindfulness is, and rediscover satisfaction and balance again.

The notion invites individuals to understand the relevance of decreasing their pace, adopting rest, and adding scheduled pauses to their lives for general health and personal growth.

One approach to decelerate and build a connection with oneself is to take pauses. It's a chance to analyze your needs, desires, and feelings. It's also a chance to recuperate and restart your activities with a new perspective.

The importance of halting occasionally

Your power to promote general welfare, personal growth, and a more balanced and fulfilling living makes pausing crucial. The following are some important explanations for the necessity of incorporating halt times in one's routine:

- Thinking and Being Present:

Pauses give a moment for contemplation and awareness. Taking a stop encourages individuals to assess their thoughts, feelings, and experiences, which increases self-awareness and a more thorough image of who they are.

- Reduced Stress:

Frequent relaxation times minimize stress and help defend against burnout. Releasing oneself from continual activity enhances mental and emotional resilience and decreases stress levels by enabling the body and mind to decompress.

- Improvements in Decision-Making

People may approach choices with clarity and a revitalized perspective when they take the time to contemplate before making them. Making more careful and informed judgments may come from this.

- Enhanced Originality:

Accepting pauses has been related to increased levels of creativity. Taking a mental vacation fosters the emergence of new thoughts, opinions, and problem-solving solutions.

- Enhanced Concentration and Output:

Taking purposeful breaks helps boost productivity and attentiveness. People who take brief pauses from their jobs could prevent mental tiredness and return to their work with new concentration and vitality.

- Improved Health Physically:

Including relaxation intervals in regular life increases physical well-being. It aids in preventing the bad repercussions of lengthy sitting, ocular tiredness, and other physical issues associated with persistent work.

- Harmonious Life:

By encouraging individuals to spend time on other parts of their well-being, such as employment, relationships, hobbies, and self-care, pause points help people lead more balanced lives.

- Improved Connections:

Taking breaks to socialize develops ties between individuals. Pause times give possibilities for profound talks and shared experiences, whether with loved ones, friends, or colleagues.

- Keeping Burnout at Bay:

It is recommended to take frequent breaks to prevent burnout. An ecologically sustainable and healthier lifestyle may be maintained by avoiding excessive effort and creating time for relaxation and recreation.

- Enhanced Contentment and Joy:

Including purposeful pauses promotes enjoyment and fulfillment with life in general. The quality of life is increased by creating time for pleasurable and gratifying activities.

- Flexibility and Sturdiness:

Pause moments allow individuals the mental space they need to deal with challenges, setbacks, or changes, which encourages resilience and adaptability. This suppleness is necessary for managing life's shocks.

- Relation between Objectives and Values:

People may re-establish their connection to their long-term ambitions and ideals by stopping. It allows the ability to analyze whether one's existing actions are in accordance with their objectives and modify them as required.

The benefits of stopping occasionally

People may benefit from taking breaks in many different aspects of their life. Here are a few key benefits:

- Reducing Stress: By allowing for relaxation, halting decreases stress levels and staves against burnout.
- Improved Welfare: Frequent breaks boost mental, emotional, and physical health, which increases overall well-being.
- Enhanced Concentration and Output: Short pauses protect the mind from growing fatigued, which promotes attention and productivity.
- Detail and Introspection: Pausing allows for reflection, which enhances decision-making and heightens self-awareness.

- Increased Creativity: Taking pauses has been related to increased levels of creativity because it stimulates the emergence of new ideas and thoughts.
- A Well-Being Lifestyle: By allocating time for work, relationships, and personal pastimes, stop points help to a balanced existence.
- Stronger Connections: Breaks allow individuals the opportunity to participate meaningfully, supporting the development of both personal and professional ties.
- Keeping Burnout at Bay: By taking planned pauses, burnout may be prevented and long-term wellness is preserved.
- More Contentment: Taking breaks to participate in pleasurable and gratifying activities boosts one's overall happiness.

- Health Benefits for the Body: By avoiding the physical strain that comes with persistent work, pauses minimize the probability of health issues.
- Self-adjustment and resilience: Frequent breaks enable the mind to assess barriers and setbacks, which encourages adaptability and resilience.
- Relationship with Objectives and Values: Taking purposeful pauses helps individuals reconfirm their principles and connect their actions to long-term aspirations.
- Improved Originality: Time spent being idle encourages creativity by promoting the creation of unique ideas and inventive solutions.
- Higher Levels of Energy: Taking breaks helps the body and mind heal, which offers one more energy for the tasks at hand.

- Enhanced Quality of Sleep: Adding pause intervals to your day decreases stress and boosts relaxation, which improves the quality of your sleep.

How to begin utilizing pause periods

Incorporating purposeful pauses for relaxation and contemplation into your everyday routine is the first step towards incorporating stop locations. This is a complete resource to aid you in establishing pause times in your life:

- Recognize the Need: Understand how vital it is to take breaks for your health. Recognize that taking purposeful pauses leads to better productivity and happiness in general.

- Determine the Trigger Points: Determine the specific occasions throughout your schedule that kick off your stress, tiredness, or overwhelming reactions. During a stressful moment, mid-morning, or after a meeting are some instances of these.
- Determined Goals: Give your pause points a distinct purpose. Making the most of these moments demands having a clear objective, whether that intention is to meditate, relax, or spend a little time doing something you prefer.
- Start Modestly: Start out with small pauses. A modest five-minute break may have a tremendous influence. It is simpler to manage and more likely to be incorporated consistently if you start modestly.

- Schedule Breaks: Schedule pause points into your calendar or set reminders on your phone. Treat these breaks with the same amount of significance as other items on your list.
- Choose Activities Wisely: Select activities that correspond with your aims for the pause. This might be a brief stroll, deep breathing exercises, stretching, or perhaps a period of silent thought.
- Create a Relaxing Environment: If feasible, provide a defined location for your pause spots. This might be a nice chair, a peaceful nook, or even an outdoor area. A suitable setting boosts the efficiency of your breaks.
- Communicate Boundaries: Communicate your desire to take pause points with coworkers, family, or anybody you connect with often.

Establishing boundaries helps ensure that these times are honored.

- Experiment and Adjust: Experiment with various activities and times for your pause spots. Pay attention to what works best for you and be open to adapt your strategy depending on your developing requirements.
- Reflect on the Benefits: Regularly reflect on the good effects of your pause spots. Notice improvements in your stress levels, productivity, and general well-being. This reinforcement promotes continuing practice.
- Encourage Others: Share your experience with friends, family, or coworkers, and urge others to include stop periods into their routines. Collective support may build a culture of well-being.
- Build Consistency: Aim for consistency in taking pause points. As it becomes a habit, you'll

discover that these purposeful pauses easily merge into your regular life, becoming a natural part of your routine.

Chapter 2

Different Types of Pause Points

They are different types of pause points which are:

Short pause points

Shortstop points are often a few seconds to a few minutes long. They may be taken throughout the day to check in with yourself and reconnect with your priorities.

Here are a few examples of brief pause points:

- Taking a few deep breaths before beginning an assignment
- Take a brief stroll around the block to clear your brain

- Pausing during a discussion to listen to what the other person is saying
- Take a minute to reflect on your day before bed

Long pause points

Long pause points are often 15 minutes or more. They may be used to relax and de-stress, to reflect on your life, or to prepare for the future.

Here are a few instances of extended pause points:

- Taking a bath or shower
- Meditating for 15-20 minutes
- Reading a book or magazine
- Going for a stroll in nature
- Journaling for 15-20 minutes

Formal pause points

Formal pause moments are often planned and prepared in advance. They may entail particular actions or ceremonies.

Here are a few instances of formal halt points:

- Attending a weekly yoga class
- Going to church or synagogue on the weekends
- Participating in a meditation group
- Having a regular treatment appointment
- Taking a vacation or sabbatical

Informal pause points

Informal halt points are spontaneous and unplanned. They may originate from the natural flow of your day or from a scenario that you are in.

Here are a few instances of informal halt points:

- Take a few minutes to relax and enjoy a cup of coffee or tea
- Chatting with a buddy or colleague
- Watching a sunset or sunrise
- Playing with your pet
- Taking a nap

Individual pause points

Individual pause points are taken alone. They are a moment to reflect on your own ideas, emotions, and needs.

Here are a few instances of specific pause points:

- Meditating Journaling
- Taking a stroll in nature
- Reading a book
- Taking a bath or shower

Group halt points

Group pause points are taken with others. They may be a time to connect with others, to learn from each other, or to just enjoy one another's company.

Here are a few examples of group pause points:

- Attending a yoga class
- Participating in a meditation group
- Going to church or synagogue on the weekends
- Having lunch with pals
- Playing board games with family

No matter what sort of stop point you use, the main thing is to stay consistent with your exercise. The more you take pause points, the more rewards you will receive.

Here are a few strategies for implementing stop times throughout your day:

- o Schedule pause points into your schedule.
- o Set up a distinct location for your pause spots.
- o Choose activities that you like and that allow you to relax and de-stress.
- o Be present and aware throughout your pause points.
- o Start small and progressively increase the amount of time you spend taking pause points each day.

Taking stop points is a simple method to boost your general well-being. So determine what works for you and start taking pause points immediately!

Chapter 3

Creating a Pause Point Routine

Creating a stop point habit requires generating purposeful periods of relaxation and refreshment in your daily calendar. In the fast-paced rhythm of contemporary life, where activity frequently takes priority, finding moments to halt and refresh becomes crucial for general well-being.

The notion of a "Pause Point Routine" concentrates upon consciously adding breaks into your daily routine, allowing time for relaxation, contemplation, and recharging. This practice is a proactive and aware way to manage the pressures of everyday life, creating balance, and boosting the quality of each moment.

By accepting deliberate pauses, you go on a path to develop a more harmonious and meaningful everyday living.

Finding the correct timing for pause points

Finding the proper time for stop points means proactively finding instances in your daily routine when purposeful pauses might be most helpful.

Consider aspects such as your natural energy levels, circadian cycles, and job activities to identify appropriate times for rest. Aligning with personal preferences, exploiting natural transitions, and responding to changes in your routine are crucial factors. By listening to your body and taking pauses during moments of lower energy or before stressful occasions, you can design a personalized pause point program that increases well-being and productivity.

The greatest moment to take pause points is when you need them. This might be at the beginning of the day, at the conclusion of the day, before a large meeting, or during a difficult scenario.

Finding the proper time for stop points requires recognizing instances in your daily routine when purposeful pauses might be most useful. Here are several ways to assist you in finding the ideal periods for pause points:

- Assess Your Natural Energy Peaks and Troughs:

Observe your energy levels throughout the day. Identify when you naturally feel more alert and concentrated (energy peaks) and when you suffer decreases in concentration or motivation (energy troughs).

- Align with Circadian Rhythms:

Consider your body's inherent circadian patterns. Many individuals endure a natural energy sag in the early afternoon. Aim to arrange pause moments during these lower-energy times.

- Sync with Work Tasks:

Integrate pause moments wisely with your job responsibilities. For instance, take a brief pause after finishing a concentrated work or before moving to a new project.

- Leverage Natural Transitions:

Utilize natural transitions in your day, such as the conclusion of a meeting, a commute, or the finish of a key assignment. These instances readily lend themselves to including a pause.

- Mid-Morning and Mid-Afternoon Breaks:

Consider including pause moments mid-morning and mid-afternoon.

These pauses might act as a refreshing respite to alleviate any lunchtime tiredness.

- Mealtime Breaks:

Align some of your pause moments with mealtimes. Taking a stop to consciously enjoy a meal not only gives physical nutrition but also acts as a mental and emotional recharge.

- Scheduled Breaks:

If your schedule permits, set particular times for breaks. This can require arranging small breaks on your calendar or utilizing built-in break intervals if you're following a planned routine.

- Align with Personal Preferences:

Consider your own interests and behaviors. Some folks may prefer a morning meditation, while others may find a post-lunch stroll more therapeutic. Tailor your pause points to what feels most natural for you.

- Consider Workload Intensity:

Assess your workload and tasks for the day. If you have extremely difficult or focused work times, arrange stop moments before and after these periods to retain attention and avoid burnout.

- Pause Before Stressful Events:

Incorporate a stop place before participating in potentially stressful or hard situations. This might help you approach these circumstances with a clearer and calmer mentality.

- Adapt to Changes in Routine:

Be flexible and alter your pause point schedule to changes in your routine. Life is dynamic, and altering your breaks based on daily differences may help maintain consistency.

- Listen to Your Body:

Pay attention to how your body and mind feel throughout the day. If you notice indicators of exhaustion, tension, or a desire for mental clarity, it can be an appropriate moment for a stop.

Choosing the proper length for pause spots

Choosing the correct duration for stop spots is vital since it directly affects the efficacy of the break. Before I provide you with a tutorial on how you may select the proper duration for stop points, let me briefly explain its significance.

The duration of a pause point should coincide with the purpose and context of the break. Too short, and it could not give adequate relaxation or repair; too long, and it might impede productivity or generate a feeling of detachment.

Selecting an adequate length ensures that the break fulfills its intended objective, whether it's to replenish energy, encourage creativity, or boost general well-being. The correct duration for stop points establishes a balance, enabling people to return to their jobs with renewed attention, productivity, and a feeling of restored clarity.

Now that I have described the necessity of picking the proper duration for pause points, Here's a step-by-step approach to assist you in deciding the best length for your pause points:

- ## Define Your Goals:

Clarify the objective of your pause spots. Whether it's to replenish energy, boost attention, or induce relaxation, knowing your aims will dictate the choice of the proper duration.

- ## Consider Task Complexity:

Assess the intricacy of the work you are taking a break from. More intellectually taxing work could benefit from somewhat longer pauses to allow for mental rejuvenation.

- ## Evaluate Your Energy Level

Tune into your natural energy rhythms throughout the day. Consider arranging lengthier breaks at moments when your energy levels tend to decrease, such as mid-afternoon.

- **Experiment with Break Durations:**

Experiment with various break durations. Start with shorter pauses, such as 5-10 minutes, and progressively adapt depending on how effectively you feel rejuvenated and ready to continue your tasks.

- **Match Breaks to Tasks:**

Match the duration of your break to the nature of the work. Routine or less difficult work may need shorter breaks, while more complicated or intellectually draining activities could benefit from somewhat longer pauses.

- **Consider Frequency:**

Determine how regularly you can integrate pause spots into your program. If you have the flexibility for shorter, more frequent breaks, or prefer longer less frequent breaks, match the length with your selected frequency.

- **Personal Preferences:**

Take your particular preferences into consideration. Some people may prefer shorter, more frequent breaks, while others may find longer pauses more refreshing. Tailor the length to what feels most comfortable for you.

- **Assess the Activity:**

Consider the sort of activity you intend to participate in during the break. hobbies like stretching or brief walks may be ideal for shorter breaks, while meditation or more immersed hobbies may benefit from a longer period.

- **Evaluate Productivity Impact:**

Assess how the specified break duration affects your production. The idea is to achieve a balance where the break boosts your efficiency and attention without contributing to a major decline in output.

- **Listen to Your Body:**

Pay attention to how your body and mind behave during and after the break. If you feel properly refreshed and ready to continue your work, the specified duration is likely acceptable.

- **Reflect on Workload:**

Consider your workload for the day. If you have intensive or lengthy work times, arrange breaks properly to minimize burnout and maintain maintained attention.

- **Adjust Based on Effectiveness:**

Periodically examine the efficiency of your specified break durations. Be open to modifying the time depending on changes in your routine, energy levels, or general well-being.

- Consider External Constraints:

Take into consideration any external restrictions, such as the availability of break areas or your office culture. Adapt your break durations to correspond with external influences as required.

- Trial and Error:

Finding the proper length generally entails some trial and error. Be patient and open to altering your approach until you achieve the perfect balance that meets your demands and increases your overall well-being.

Creating a suitable environment for pause points.

Creating a pleasant location for stop periods is vital since it considerably boosts the efficacy of the break. A cozy setting encourages rest and enables people to completely detach from the responsibilities of their work. It fosters an atmosphere that is beneficial to both physical and mental renewal, making the break experience more purposeful. A pleasant environment, whether it's an outdoor area, a special nook, or a nice chair, makes it easier to relax, refuel, and resume tasks with more clarity and concentration. Making pause points a worthwhile and long-lasting part of one's routine depends critically on the setting.

This is a step-by-step approach to help you create a comfortable and welcoming space for your breaks:

- Determine the Optimal Environment:

Think about your tastes and decide what kind of setting best suits your needs to feel relaxed and at ease. Select a location that speaks to you, whether it's a peaceful nook, a beloved chair, or an outside area.

- Eliminate the Mess:

To make the selected area seem tidy and well-organized, declutter it. Eliminating extraneous objects promotes a calmer atmosphere by lowering distractions.

- Include Cozy Seating:

Make an investment in cozy seating alternatives. Whether it's a comfortable chair, pillows, or a blanket, make sure the setting promotes ease and relaxation.

- Add Your Own Touches:

Put your own stamp on the area to make it really yours.

Accent your space with things that make you happy, such as peaceful artwork, plants, or your best novels. Customizing the area makes it even more cozy.

- Think About Lighting

Select lights based on your own taste. If you can't get natural light, go for warm, soft artificial lighting instead. Steer clear of intense, glaring lighting that might be uncomfortable.

- Boost Ambience

Think about adding components that improve the room's atmosphere. You may create a relaxing ambiance at your pause points with soft music, aromatherapy, or quiet nature sounds.

- Temperature Management:

Make sure it's a comfortable temperature. If at all feasible, change the temperature of the area you've selected to suit your tastes.

You may do this by turning on a fan, changing the thermostat, or opening the windows to let in some fresh air.

- Add Comfortable Textures:

Add soft furniture, blankets, and cushions to create a pleasant atmosphere. It is more comfortable and relaxing all around to create a tactile and welcoming environment.

- Privacy Aspects to Consider:

If the area you've selected is communal, think about privacy. To provide a feeling of privacy during your break, set limits or utilize furniture such as room dividers.

- Availability of Calming Instruments:

Maintain your relaxation resources close at hand. Having a diary, a meditation app, or a favorite book close at hand guarantees that you may easily partake in relaxing activities.

- **IT-Free Area:**

If at all feasible, make your halt point area a tech-free zone. Reduce the amount of electronics in the room to foster a more peaceful atmosphere and to encourage a vacation from screens.

- **Continual Upkeep:**

Maintain and refresh your pause point space on a regular basis. To make sure it continues to be a welcoming haven for your breaks, keep it tidy, orderly, and visually attractive.

- **Assess and Modify:**

Review your pause point space's efficacy on a regular basis. Be willing to make changes and improvements if certain components aren't helping you feel comfortable or at ease anymore.

Choosing things to for your pause points

You may engage in a wide range of activities during your pause periods. Select enjoyable pursuits that promote relaxation and stress relief for yourself.

You may utilize the following activities as your pause points:

- Breathing Techniques:

To ease tension and calm your thoughts, engage in conscious, deep breathing. Breathe in deeply through your nose, hold it for a little while, and then gently release the air through your mouth.

- Flexibility or Yoga:

Use yoga poses or light stretching to help you become more flexible and relieve physical stress. Pay attention to places that tend to become tight while you're working.

- **Fast Meditation**

Take a little meditation session to declutter your thoughts and develop a sensation of serenity. Use applications that provide guided meditation or basic mindfulness exercises.

- **Go for a Quick Walk:**

Take a little stroll outdoors, particularly if you've been sitting still for a while. Your body and mind may be revitalized by exercise and fresh air.

- **Play some music:**

To create a relaxing ambiance, play music that is uplifting or comforting. For a few minutes, close your eyes and lose yourself in the music.

- **Be Alert Observation:**

Take time to observe with awareness.

Concentrate on an item in your immediate surroundings and take note of its features, hues, and textures. This easy exercise may improve awareness.

- Read a Poetry or Short Article:

Keep a file of brief essays or poetry that you find thought-provoking or inspirational. Take a moment to read a short piece and consider what it means.

- Writing a Journal:

Take a few minutes to write down your sentiments, ideas, and things for which you are thankful in a diary. Keeping a journal may be a healing tool for gaining perspective and processing feelings.

- Picture Language:

Shut your eyes and picture a serene location, such as a forest or beach. To unwind, lose yourself in the minutiae of this mental picture.

- Savor a Nutritious Snack:

To fuel your body during your break, have a modest, wholesome food. Pick a food that gives you energy for a longer period of time, such as yogurt, almonds, or fruits.

- Relationship with Others:

Establish a quick chat with a friend or coworker. Social contacts, whether face-to-face or over the phone, may give you a great emotional lift.

- Rapid Expression of Creativity:

Take up a quick creative endeavor, like drawing, doodling, or composing a few verses of poetry. This might help clear your head and inspire creativity.

- Technology-Free Quiet:

Accept a few quiet minutes without using any electronics. Encourage inner peace by finding a peaceful place to sit and allowing your thoughts to relax.

- Box breathing or breathwork:

To control your breathing and encourage relaxation, try out some breathwork methods, such as box breathing.

- Gratitude-based statements:

To improve your attitude and foster a good mentality, repeat inspirational quotes or positive affirmations.

- Easy Desk Activities:

To release physical strain, try some easy desk exercises like ankle circles, shoulder rolls, and neck stretches.

- Pause for aromatherapy:

To create a relaxing ambiance, use scented candles or essential oils. Take time to enjoy the sensory experience and breathe in the calming aromas.

- **Simple Brain Teaser or Puzzle:**

Try your brain with a quick brainteaser or puzzle. This may be an engaging and enjoyable method to change your attention.

- **Gratitude Thought:**

Consider the things for which you are thankful. Spend time cultivating thankfulness by acknowledging the good things in your life.

- **Focus Visualization:**

Imagine yourself finishing a job or project effectively. Motivation and attention may both be improved by this vision.

Select pursuits that you find meaningful and that fit the particular objectives of your rest periods. Try out a variety of activities to see which ones are most beneficial to your productivity and overall well-being.

In order to overcome stop point reluctance, you must address typical roadblocks that may make it difficult for you to schedule breaks into your schedule.

Potential obstacles that may arise while using Pause Points and the techniques to get around them:

1. Sensational Lack of Time:
- Difficulty: Feeling too occupied to take breaks.
- Solution: Make self-care a priority by understanding that taking breaks increases focus and output. Put stop times on your calendar so that they become an essential component of your daily routine.
2. Occupational Culture:
- Challenge is an anti-break corporate culture.
- Solution: Make the case for the importance of breaks in raising productivity and overall well-being.

Discuss the benefits of utilizing pause moments with colleagues, and collaborate to create a welcoming environment at work.

3. Sense of Guilt:
- Challenge: Feeling of guilt over taking pauses.
- Solution: Recognize that in order to maintain peak performance, breaks are essential. Realize that taking care of your health benefits your work and changes the way you see things.

4. Absence of Knowledge:
- Challenge: Lack of knowledge about the benefits of pausing.
- Solution: educate yourself and others on the benefits of taking breaks for mental well-being, output, and general job satisfaction. Provide relevant study findings and case studies.

5. Observed Inefficiency:
- Problem: I think that there won't be any impact from pause spots.
- Solution: Take short, sensible breaks at first to see how well they affect your focus and level of energy. You'll probably start to notice the benefits over time and become more motivated to keep going.
6. Fear of Getting Lagged:
- Challenge: Worry that taking pauses may cause you to fall behind on your responsibilities.
- Solution: Acknowledge that taking regular pauses may help you stay productive and prevent burnout, which will ultimately lead to sustainable production. To attain a good balance, strategically schedule your breaks and household tasks.

7. Absence of Rest Periods
- Problem: There are no designated stop sites.
- Solution is to designate a specific location for stopping, even if it's only a little area inside your desk. Talk to individuals about the importance of having rest areas in communal areas.
8. Cultural Preferences:
- Challenge lies in cultural norms that place a premium on perpetual activity.
- Solution: Promote a cultural shift by emphasizing the value of well-being and work-life balance. Set a positive example by demonstrating the advantages of taking regular pauses.
9. Intricacy Eliminating:
- Difficulty putting aside work during breaks as a challenge.

- Solution: During your pause times, establish boundaries by turning off work-related communications and putting up physical or digital barriers. Make use of this opportunity to engage in mentally calming activities.

10. Physique Soreness:

- Challenge: Pain prevents me from unwinding during breaks.
- Solution: Get rid of physical discomfort by adding stretching exercises, buying ergonomic furniture, or going for short walks. Pause places work better when the ambiance is nice.

11. Unhelpful Coworkers:

- Difficulty: Working with coworkers who don't believe in taking breaks.
- Solution: Inform your coworkers about the benefits of taking breaks and how they create a more positive and effective work atmosphere. Promote a shift in the collective

mindset to place a higher value on well-being.

12.   Unreliable Routine:

- Problem: Not always include pause times in your schedule.
- Solution: Schedule frequent breaks into your schedule and make them a regular aspect of your day. Be intentional in identifying these times of halt and set reminders for yourself.

Chapter 5

Using Pause Points to Lead a More Meaningful Life

Lowering tension

Using stop points has several benefits, one of which is that they might help reduce stress. Our bodies go into fight-or-flight mode when we are nervous. This is a survival tactic that helps us deal with danger. Our bodies, however, are unable to cope with constant anxiety. Numerous health issues, such as anxiety, sadness, and heart disease, might result from this. Taking breaks from stress allows our bodies to recuperate and relax, which helps break the cycle of stress. We slow down our respiration and heart rate when we take pauses.

By doing this, the quantity of stress hormones in our bodies is reduced.

Increasing output

Adopting stop points may seem counterintuitive, but they might really help to increase productivity. Our minds become tired from constant activity, and we begin to make mistakes. Making stops gives our brains a chance to unwind and regenerate. Increased focus, inventiveness, and attention to detail may result from this. According to one study, employees who took regular breaks were more productive than those who didn't. Additionally, the study showed that employees who took breaks had a lower risk of burnout.

Increasing originality

Pauses might also help to improve creativity. We are more likely to generate original thoughts and solutions when we are at ease and have unrestricted access to our minds. According to one study, those who took breaks to daydream were more creative than people who didn't. Additionally, the study showed that daydreamers were more likely to generate original and novel ideas.

Fostering stronger connections

Pause periods might also strengthen bonds. People trust and feel closer to us when we take the time to engage with them. We also get to know one another and our needs better. According to one study, couples who engaged in conversation with each other on a regular basis reported more satisfaction in their marriages than those who didn't take breaks. Additionally, the poll found that couples who connected had a higher chance of sticking together.

Fulfilling your goals

Pauses might also help you accomplish your goals. You're more likely to succeed when you take the time to reflect on your goals and devise a plan of action to achieve them. According to one study, those who often stopped to set goals and develop plans to reach them had a higher chance of success than people who didn't take breaks. The poll also revealed that those who developed plans and objectives were generally happier with their lives.

Resources for Taking Pause Points

I have done extensive research, selected a few useful resources, and am recommending these tools and resources to assist you in finding and implementing effective strategies for incorporating breaks into your routine if you would want to learn more and go deeper:

Articles and Websites:

- Mindful: Resources and articles about mindfulness, including tips for taking thoughtful breaks, may be found at mindful.org.
- Review of Harvard Business: The Harvard Business Review has a number of articles on maintaining work-life balance, productivity, and the benefits of taking breaks.
- Psychology Today: Psychology Today: Offers information on the

mental health benefits of pausing and caring for oneself.
- Greater Good Science Center
- The Center for Mindful Self-Compassion

Podcasts

- Podcasts: Meryl Arnett's "The Mindful Minute" examines a variety of aspects of mindfulness and provides short guided meditations that you can include in your breaks.
- Podcast: "The Art of Charm" episodes such as "The Power of Mindful Walking" go into doable tactics for pausing and incorporating mindfulness into your daily routine.

Online courses:

Coursera: Yale University's "The Science of Well-Being" course on Coursera examines the science of happiness and well-being, emphasizing the value of relaxation and self-care.

- "Mindfulness Practices" on LinkedIn Learning, written by Arianna Huffington discusses ideas for using mindfulness exercises in daily life to improve wellbeing in general.

Programs for the Workplace: Employee Assistance Programs (EAPs): EAPs, which provide tools and support for workers' well-being, including strategies for taking breaks, are offered by a lot of companies.

Wellness Programs: Programs for workplace wellness often include resources and activities centered on stress management, mindfulness, and the need to take breaks.

Apps:

Headspace

Calm

Insight Timer

Conclusion

Dear friend including intentional rest periods in your schedule is essential for preserving both overall well-being and productivity. The abundance of options from research-backed remedies to mindfulness exercises highlights the importance of taking breaks. Identifying and addressing the problems is the first step in creating a culture that values and encourages stop points. Overcoming obstacles like as perceived time constraints, managing work obligations, or cultivating the practice of disconnecting are significantly outweighed by the benefits.

Through an examination of the diverse range of provided information, you may tailor your strategy to suit your own needs and preferences. These resources, which range from books and articles to workplace initiatives and programs, provide helpful suggestions and doable methods for easily implementing stop moments into your daily activities.

Remember that every individual has a different path to optimal well-being. Seize the opportunity to try out a variety of strategies so that you may finally establish a routine that aligns with your goals and enhances your personal and professional lives. Taking breaks from work is more than just vacationing; it's an intentional investment in your long-term growth and

www.ingramcontent.com/pod-product-compliance
Lightning Source LLC
Chambersburg PA
CBHW071103260726
48661CB00006B/2423